GOD'S FLOWER

Maria Garford

Copyright © 2008 by Maria Garford

Bible quotations are from the
Good News Bible
© 1976, 1979
by the American Bible Society

ISBN 0-9538087-3-4

Published by Maria Garford
45 Ramsdell Road,
Fleet, Hants GU51 1DE
England

Printed at St. Paul Press Training School,
Bandra, Mumbai 400 050.
INDIA.

DEDICATED TO

My nephews, nieces,

their spouses and their children

Gustavo Adolfo, Lara and Gustavo

Manuel Eduardo, Ana Isabel and Gabriel

Graciela, Manuel, Manuel and Claudia

Henry Alex, Yomaira and Valeria

Michelle, David, Charles and Luke

Andres

Simon

AND EVERYONE CALLED PEREZ WITH LOVE

ACKNOWLEDGEMENTS

Thanks to **David** for reading the manuscript and making suggestions to improve it.

Thanks for **my family and friends,** who have prayed for this book to be anointed and to become a reality.

Thanks to **St. Paul's Press** for printing this book.

And most of all – thanks to the Holy Spirit for using me to write this book.

ALL PRAISE AND GLORY TO GOD

CONTENTS

Chapter 1

BLESSINGS AND CURSES

Have you ever wondered why a country as small as New Jersey should be in the news non-stop for all of our life time?

Which country I am writing about? I will give you a hint: the one God has chosen for His people.

ISRAEL

How do we know that God has chosen Israel? It is written inside **every** Bible in the world.

In Genesis, the first book in the Bible, chapter 12 starting on verses 1 and 2 say, *The Lord said to Abram, "Leave your country, your relatives, and your father's home, and go to a land that I am going to show you. I will give you many descendants, and they will become a great nation. I will bless you and make your name famous, so that you will be a blessing.*

Genesis 12:v 3,

*"I will bless those who bless you,
But I will curse those who curse you.
And through you I will bless all the nations."*

Any one of us receiving a request to uproot and go somewhere else would be full of questions and thinking only if I like where you are sending me, will I go. Abram believed in obeying God, so at age 75 he left and took his wife Sarai and his nephew Lot and all their possessions. They went to Canaan (the land which is now Israel) Abram travelled to the land until he arrived at the sacred tree of Moreh, the holy place at Shechem. In Genesis chapter 12 verses 7-9, *The Lord appeared to Abram and said to him,* *"This is the country that I am going to give to your descendants. Then Abram built an altar there to the Lord, who had appeared to him. After that, he moved on south to the hill country east of the city of Bethel on the west and Ai on the east. There also he built an altar and worshipped the Lord. Then he moved on from place to place, going towards the southern part of Canaan."*

As there was a famine in Canaan, Abram went farther south to Egypt to live there for a while. After he came back from Egypt, he moved from place to place going towards Bethel. He reached the place between Bethel and Ai where he had camped before and had built an altar. There he worshipped the Lord.

Abram and Lot prospered and soon had so many

animals that there was not enough pasture land for the two of them to stay together. Consequently Abram asked Lot to move to a different area of his choosing. Lot choose the most fertile land in the Jordan Valley and Abram moved to Hebron.

Genesis 13 verses 14-18 says: ..."*The Lord said to Abram, "From where you are, look carefully in all directions. I am going to give you and your descendants all the land that you see, and it will be yours for ever."* *I am going to give you so many descendants that no one will be able to count them all; it would be as easy to count all the specks of dust on earth! Now, go and look over the whole land, because I am going to give it all to you." So Abram moved his camp and settled near the sacred trees of Mamre at Hebron, and there he built an altar to the Lord."*

The Bible says that the 4 kings of Babylonia, Ellasar, Elam and Goiim went to war with 5 other kings from Sodom, Gomorrah, Admah, Zeboiim and Bela. The 4 kings won and took away everything in Sodom and Gomorrah including Lot, Abram's nephew. Genesis 14:14-16, "*When Abram heard that his nephew had been captured, he called together all the fighting men in his camp, 318 in all, and pursued the four kings all the way to Dan. There he divided his men into groups, attacked the enemy by night, and defeated them.*

He chased them as far as Hobah, north of Damascus, and recovered the loot that had been taken. He also brought back, his nephew Lot and his possessions, together with the women and the other prisoners.

Genesis continues 14:17-20, *"When Abram came back from his victory over Chedorlaomer and the other kings, the king of Sodom went out to meet him in the Valley of Shaveh (also called the Kings, Valley). And Melchizedek, who was king of Salem and also a priest of the Most High God, brought bread and wine to Abram, blessed him, and said, "May the Most High God, who made heaven and earth, bless Abram! May the most High God, who gave you victory over your enemies, be praised!" And Abram gave Melchizedek a tenth of all the loot they recovered."*

The King of Sodom told Abram that he could keep the loot, but he wanted back all of his people. Abram said that he would not keep anything, not even a thread of a sandal strap otherwise the King of Sodom could brag that he was responsible for Abram's wealth, but he asked that his allies, Aner, Eshcol and Mamre should take their share.

Abram put his trust in the Lord and the Lord said to him in Genesis chapter 15 verse 7, *"I am the Lord, who led you out of Ur in Babylonia, to give you this land as your own."*

Abram asked the Lord how he would know that the land would be his and God asked for a sacrifice of a cow, a goat and a ram 3 years old and a dove and a pigeon. This Abram did. In Genesis 15:13-16 the Lord said, *"Your descendants will be strangers in a foreign land; they will be slaves there and will be treated cruelly for 400 years. But I will punish the nation that enslaves them, and when they leave that foreign land, they will take great wealth with them. You yourself will live to a ripe old age, die in peace, and be buried. It will be four generations before your descendants come back here, because I will not drive out the Amorites until they become so wicked that they must be punished."* (The Bible is full of prophecies that become true. This one became a reality when the Israelites left Egypt with Moses. The Amorites were people who occupied the country west of the Euphrates from the second half of the 3rd millennium BC).

Genesis Chapter 15 verses 17-20, *"When the sun had set and it was dark, a smoking firepot and a flaming torch suddenly appeared and passed between the pieces of the animals. Then and there the Lord made a covenant with Abram. He said,* **I promise to give your descendants all this land from the border of Egypt to the River Euphrates,** *including the lands of the Kenites, the Kenizzites, the Kadmonites, the Hittites, the Perizzites, the Rephaim, the Amorites, the Canaanites, the Girgashites, and the Jebusites."*

Chapter 2

ABRAHAM, ISAAC
AND JACOB

Abram's wife Sarai was barren so she asked Abram to sleep with her Egyptian servant girl and have a baby for Sarai. Ishmael was born when Abram was 86 years old.

When Abram was 99 years old, God appeared again and said that as Abram will be the father of many nations, his name was changed to Abraham and Sarai would be called Sarah. In Genesis 17 verses 7-8, *"I will keep my promise to you and to your descendants in future generations as an everlasting covenant. I will be your God and the God of your descendants. I will give to you and to your descendants this land in which you are now a foreigner. The whole land of Canaan will belong to your descendants for ever, and I will be their God."*

When Sarah was 90 years old, Abraham asked if Ishmael could be his heir. Genesis 17:19 says "But God said, "**No.** Your wife Sarah will bear a son and you will name him Isaac. **I will keep my covenant with him and with his descendants for ever. It is an everlasting covenant.**

Genesis 17:20 says, *"I have heard your request about Ishmael, so I will bless him and give him many children and many descendants. He will be the father of twelve princes, and I will make a great nation of his descendants.*

Genesis 17:21 says, *"But I will keep my covenant with your son Isaac, who will be born to Sarah about this time next year."* (Isaac was born as predicted.)

Abimelech went to meet Abraham and said that he could see that God was with him and everything he did and asked for peace between them. Abraham agreed, but said that the servants of Abimelech had stolen a well. Abimelech said that he was unaware of it.

Genesis 21:30-34, *"Abraham answered, "Accept these seven lambs. By doing this, you admit that I am the one who dug this well." And so the place was called Beersheba, because it was there that the two of them made a vow.*

After they had made this agreement at Beersheba, Abimelech and Phicol went back to Philistia. Then Abraham planted a tamarisk tree in Beersheba and worshipped the Lord, the Everlasting God. Abraham lived in Philistia for a long time.

Some time later God tested Abraham.

Genesis 22:2, *"Take you son, God said, your only son, Isaac, whom you love so much, and go to the*

15

land of Moriah. *There on a mountain that I will show you, offer him as a sacrifice to me.*"

Abraham did as he was told; he took the wood, his son Isaac and two servants. They travelled for 3 days. Abraham asked the servants to wait and Isaac carried the wood.

Genesis 22:9-12, *"When they came to the place which God had told him about, Abraham built an altar and arranged the wood on it. He tied up his son and placed him on the altar on top of the wood. Then he picked up the knife to kill him. But the angel of the Lord called to him from heaven, "Abraham, Abraham!" He answered, "Yes, here I am." Don't hurt the boy or do anything to him," he said. "Now I know that you honour and obey God, because you have not kept back your only son from him."*

Genesis 22:13, *Abraham looked round and saw a ram caught in a bush by its horns. He went and got it and offered it as a burnt offering instead of his son."*

When Sarah was 127 years old she died. Abraham paid 400 pieces of silver for a field, which contained the Machpelah cave where Sarah was buried. Genesis 23 verses 17-18 explain, *"That is how the property which had belonged to Ephron at Machpelah, east of Mamre, became Abraham's". It included the field, the cave which was in it, and all the trees in the field up to the edge of the property. It was recognized as*

16

Abraham's property by all the Hittities who were there at the meeting.

(Also buried there were Abraham, Rebecca, Isaac, Leah and Jacob.)

So every Bible has the proof that a field and a cave belonged to Abraham and his descendants: the Jews, and that God wants the Jews to have this land.

It is also written in **every** Bible that Abram travelled the whole length of the land of Palestine from Ur in the east to Egypt and from the south all the way to Damascus and he worshipped the Lord everywhere he went.

Abraham's son Isaac grew up, married Rebecca and had twins Esau and Jacob.

God's promise to Isaac

In Genesis 26:1-5, *"There was another famine in the land besides the earlier one during the time of Abraham. Isaac went to Abimelech, king of the Philistines, at Gerar. The Lord appeared to Isaac and said, "Do not go to Egypt, stay in this land, where I tell you to stay. Live here, and I will be with you and bless you.* I am going to give you all this territory to you and to your descendants. *I will keep the promise I made to your father Abraham. I will give you as many descendants as there are stars in the sky;* and I will give them all this territory. *All the* nations will ask me to bless them as I have blessed your descendants. I will bless you, because Abraham obeyed me and kept all my laws and commands.

God's promise to Jacob

In Genesis 28:13-15, "And there was the Lord standing beside him. "I am the Lord, the God of Abraham and Isaac, he said. "I will give to you and to your descendants this land on which you are lying. They will be as numerous as the specks of dust on the earth. They will extend their territory in all directions, and through you and your descendants I will bless all the nations. Remember I will be with you and protect you wherever you go, and I will bring you back to this land. I will not leave you until I have done all that I have promised you."

Every Bible has the proof that God promised the land to Abraham and his descendants; He again promised it to Abraham's son Isaac and his descendants; and a third time, God promised the land to Isaac's son Jacob and his descendants.

In Genesis 32:28.... "Your name will no longer be Jacob. You have struggled with God and with men, and you have won; so your name will be Israel."

Israel (Jacob) had 12 sons so they became the heads of the Twelve tribes of Israel.

Chapter 3

JOSEPH

Jacob, now named Israel gave a coat of many colours to his favourite son, Joseph, who was always having dreams of grandeur. His brothers became jealous and sold him into slavery into Egypt.

Joseph initially had favour in Egypt, but was put in prison after being falsely accused. Pharaoh had a dream that no one could interpret and Joseph was able to tell him that the dream meant that Egypt would have 7 years of plenty followed by 7 years of drought. Pharaoh was so pleased to receive the interpretation that he made Joseph the second most powerful man in the land and asked him to be in charge of saving the food for the years of drought. This he did.

After 7 years, the famine was also felt in Canaan and Jacob asked his sons to go to Egypt to buy grain. This they did, but did not recognise that the second most powerful man in Egypt was their brother whom they had sold. Joseph convinced them that the famine would last for 7 years and to bring their father to Egypt. 70 of Israel's family came and settled in Goshen because they were shepherds.

In the course of time Joseph, his brothers, and all the rest of that generation died, but their descendants, the Israelites had many children and became so numerous and strong that Egypt was filled with them.

In Genesis 49:1-28, Jacob, now named Israel, gave each of his sons a special blessing and this is what he said about Judah in Genesis 49:10, *"Judah will hold the royal sceptre, And his descendants will always rule. Nations will bring him tribute and bow in obedience before him.* Each son received the blessings of the covenant of Abraham.

Chapter 4

MOSES

When a new Egyptian King, who knew nothing about Joseph, came to power, he decided to put slave drivers over the Jews to crush their spirits with hard labour.

Genesis 15:16, *"It will be four generations before your descendants come back here, because I will not drive out the Amorites until they become so wicked that they must be punished."*

The King of Egypt asked the midwives to kill the boy children when they were helping the Hebrew women, but the midwives feared God and did not do it. When the Israelites became even more numerous, the king issued a command to all his people to take every newborn Hebrew boy and throw him into the Nile, but let all the girls live.

God decided it was time for the Jews to leave Egypt, He asked Moses to be His spokesman. Moses said that he was not an eloquent speaker so Aaron, his brother was asked to go with Moses. Aaron and Moses went to Pharaoh to ask him to let the Israelites leave Egypt. Pharaoh wanted the Israelites to continue to build his cities so he refused to let the Israelites go. God smite the Egyptians with plagues representing their gods, which proved that God was more powerful than their gods:

1. The river Nile's water was turned into blood
2. A plague of frogs
3. A plague of gnats
4. A plague of flies
5. Death of the animals
6. A plague of boils on the Egyptian's faces and bodies.
7. A plague of hail
8. A plague of locusts
9. Darkness for 3 days – the sun did not shine.
10. The death of their first born to humans and cattle.

None of these plagues affected the Israelites as they worshipped the true God.

After the death of his first born child, Pharaoh relented and let the Israelites go. There were about 600,000 men not counting the women or the children.

When the Israelites had left, Pharaoh changed his mind and went after them. The Israelites had reached the Red Sea and through a miracle of God who parted the sea, they were able to walk right through the gap, but when the Egyptians tried to follow, the Red Sea closed and they all died.

(Some people are always trying to dispute the accuracy of the Bible: one teacher decided to explain that the red sea that year was only 1 ft.

high of water that is why they could reach the other side. One of the pupils said that if this was true then the miracle is even greater as all the Egyptians who were following them drowned in 1 ft of water!)

God gave Moses the 10 Commandments for the Jews to obey:

1. I am the God who brought you out of Egypt when you were slaves. Worship no God, but me.
2. Do not make images of idols
3. Do not use my name in vain.
4. Observe the Sabbath and keep it holy
5. Respect your Father and your Mother
6. Do not commit murder
7. Do not commit adultery
8. Do not steal
9. Do not accuse anyone falsely
10. Do not desire any man' wife or their possessions

The Israelites were also given rules of hygiene that only two centuries later became common practice in the rest of the world.

The miracles continued when Joshua led them into the Promised Land (the land of Israel), which was divided between each of the tribes each one receiving a portion of the land.

A series of Judges ruled over Israel for a period of about four hundred and fifty years. Then

Saul, who was from the tribe of Benjamin, became their first king.

David, who was from the tribe of Judah, became the next King of Israel, followed by Solomon, whose reputation for being very wise was renowned.

Although the Jews lived in Israel and saw the power of God in miracles, they started worshipping the idols of Baal and Ashtaroth and even sacrificed their children as burnt offerings to Baal. Both the northern tribes of Israel and the southern tribes of Judah and Benjamin had to face the consequences of their sins. The nation of Assyria began carrying away the northern tribes of Israel in 722 and 721 B.C. and King Nebuchadnezzar invaded Judea, captured Jerusalem and destroyed its temple. He carried the tribe of Judah away to Babylon around 586 B.C.

The Jews did not return to Jerusalem until they had spent 70 years in captivity.

Chapter 5

EXTERMINATION

The enemy of God has always wanted to exterminate the Jews and has tried many times with no success! In the Old Testament there are two instances mentioned:

A. ESTHER

In the book of Esther, we read that King Xerses was the ruler of Persia and he promoted a man named Haman to the position of Prime Minister. The king ordered all the officials to show their respect for Haman by kneeling and bowing to him. They all did this except Mordecai who refused to do it. Mordecai was a Jew and he would only bow down to God. This made Haman very furious and he decided not only to punish Mordecai, but to kill every Jew in the whole Persian Empire. Haman asked King Xerses to sign a proclamation that on the 13th day of Adar all the Jews living in the 127 provinces from India to Ethiopia were to be slaughtered without mercy and their belonging confiscated. On hearing this, the Jews in the Capital, Susa, who knew that Esther was going to talk to the King, fasted and prayed for 3 days and nights. Esther the Queen, who was a Jew, went to see the King. This was very dangerous because the punishment for anyone who goes to the King without being summoned was death. The King was astonished to find that his proclamation meant not only the death of his queen, but also the death of her uncle Mordecai, who had once saved his life by informing him of a plot of kill him. As a proclamation signed by a Persian king could not be revoked, he agreed that the Jews could protect themselves on that day. So their grief and despair was turned into joy and happiness and this event is celebrated as a national holiday called Purim.

God found a way to save His people and to reward Mordecai:

BLESSING : In Esther 10:3 it says, *"Mordecai the Jew was second in rank only to King Xerses himself. He was honoured and well liked by his fellow-Jews. He worked for the good of his people and for the security of all their descendants."*

"I will bless those who bless you."

Is this just a coincidence?

CURSE : Esther 9:25. ... *"Haman suffered the fate he had planned for the Jews – he and his sons were hanged from the gallows"*

B. KING JEHOSHAPHAT

This is another instance written in the Bible when the nations around Israel gathered to annihilate it:

In 2 Chronicles chapter 20, it states that the armies of Moab, Ammon and Edom gathered together and were marching towards Judah. When King Jehoshaphat heard of it, he ordered that a fast should be observed throughout the country. God spoke through a Levite called Jahaziel who said, *"The Lord says that you must not be discouraged or be afraid to face this large army. The battle depends on God, not on you. Attack them tomorrow as they come up the pass at Ziz. You will meet them at the end of the valley that leads to the wild country near Jeruel. You will not have to fight this battle. Just take up your positions and wait; you will see the Lord give you victory. People of Judah and Jerusalem, do not hesitate or be afraid. Go out to battle, and the Lord will be with you!"* (2 Chronicles 20:15-17) King Jehoshaphat believed God implicitly so he sent the army but with a big difference, he put the musicians in front to sing praises to God on their way. When they began to sing, the Lord threw the invading armies into chaos and they started fighting amongst themselves. When the Israelite army arrived they found everyone dead. God had won the victory.

BLESSING : The Israelites won the battle by trusting God and singing. Not one man was hurt.

Is this just a coincidence?

CURSE : Invading armies just killed each other. *"I will curse those who curse you."*

Is this just a coincidence?

27

Chapter 6

JESUS

God waited for the time to be right to send His Son to redeem us as God had a contact point when Abraham was willing to sacrifice his son Isaac in obedience to God. Jesus was born in the land of Israel and had the following Jewish ancestors as written in the Bible in the book of Matthew chapter 1-17, *"This is the list of the ancestors of Jesus Christ, a descendant of David, who was a descendant of Abraham.*

From Abraham to King David, the following ancestors are listed: Abraham, Isaac, Jacob, Judah and his brothers, then Perez and Zerah, Hezron, Ram, Amminadab, Nahshon, Salmon, Boaz, Obed, Jesse and King David.

From David to the time when the people of Israel were taken into exile in Babylon, the following ancestors are listed: David, Solomon, Rehoboam, Abijah, Asa, Jehoshaphat, Jehoram, Ahaz, Hezekiah, Manasseh, Amon, Josiah and Jehoiachin and his brothers.

From the time after the exile in Babylon to the birth of Jesus, the following ancestors are listed: Jehoiachin, Shealtiel, Zerubbabel, Abiud, Eliakim, Azor, Zadok, Achim, Eliud, Eleazar, Matthan, Jacob and Joseph who married Mary, the mother of Jesus, who was called the Messiah.

So then there were 14 generations from Abraham to David, and 14 from David to the exile in Babylon and 14 from then to the birth of the Messiah."

Jesus lived the life of a Jew by being circumcised when he was 8 days old and by traveling to Jerusalem when he was 12 years old to celebrate the Feast of the Passover. During his Ministry, He taught in the Synagogues. The 12 disciples were all Jews.

The Jewish leaders at the time did not accept him as they expected the Messiah to help them with their immediate problems i.e., the Roman occupation. God was thinking of eternity and as He is a just judge, He could not let human kind get away free without paying for their sins, someone had to pay the price, so like a loving parent to the people of the world, He sent his Son to do it. A death in the electric chair or by hanging would have been easier on Jesus, but God did not choose such a quick death as the sins of the world were enormous. God also wanted us healthy so Jesus was whipped for us to be healed by the wounds he received.

Everything Jesus did was written in the Bible before it happened:

1) That He would be born of a Virgin. He was.

2) That He would be in Bethlehem. He was

3) That He would come out of Egypt. His

parents took him to Egypt to flee from Herod, who wanted to kill him.

4) That He would be a Nazarene. (He grew up in Nazareth).

5) That He would work miracles. He did

 a) Jesus healed many people (Simon Peter's Mother-in-law with a fever; a man with a dreaded skin disease; a paralysed man; a man with a paralysed hand; a man with evil spirits; the woman with severe bleeding for 12 years; the sick in Gennesaret; a deaf-mute; a blind man; an epileptic boy; blind Bartimaeus; a man born blind; two blind men; a man with crippled hand; a man with swollen arms and legs; an officer's servant; a paralysed man in Capernaum; a paralysed man in Jerusalem; a slave of the High Priest; the son of an official; ten men with skin disease; etc. etc. etc.

 b) Water turned into wine

 c) Jesus calms a storm

 d) Jesus feeds a great crowd twice

 e) Jesus walks on water

 f) Jesus raised the dead: the 12 year old daughter of Jairus; the son of the widow of Nain, and Lazarus

 g) A coin in a fish's mouth;

 h) Cursing the fig tree which died

 i) A great catch of fish twice

5) That He would die.

This was written 700 years before it actually happened in Isaiah 53:3-8, *"We despised him and rejected him; he endured suffering and pain. No one would even look at him – we ignored him as if he were nothing. But he endured the suffering that should have been ours, the pain that we should have borne. All the while we thought that his suffering was punishment sent by God. But because of our sins he was wounded, beaten because of the evil we did. We are healed by the punishment he suffered, made whole by the blows he received. All of us were like sheep that were lost, each of us going his own way. But the Lord made the punishment fall on him, the punishment all of us deserved. He was treated harshly, but endured it humbly; he never said a word. Like a lamb about to be slaughtered, like a sheep about to be sheared, he never said a word. He was arrested and sentenced and led off to die, and no one cared about his fate. He was put to death for the sins of our people."* Thank you Jesus for being our Redeemer and Saviour.

Peter explained it this way in his first letter chapter 2 verses 22-25, *"He committed no sin, and no one ever heard a lie come from his lips. When he was insulted, he did not answer back with an insult; when he suffered, he did not threaten, but placed his hopes in God, the righteous*

Judge. Christ himself carried our sins in his body to the cross, so that we might die to sin and live for righteousness. It is by his wounds that we have been healed. You were like sheep that had lost their way, but now you have been brought back to follow the Shepherd and Keeper of your souls."

People believe that the Jews are under a curse because some of the Jews who were in Jerusalem accepted the suggestion of their religious leaders to demand that Jesus be crucified. The curse was lifted immediately on the cross when Jesus said, *"Forgive them, Father! They don't know what they are doing"* (Luke 23:34). So God took away the curse on the Jews that same day.

6) That Jesus would rise from the dead 3 days later.

His tomb is empty as Luke 24:6-7, *"He is not here; he has been raised. Remember what he said to you while he was in Galilee: 'The Son of Man must be handed over to sinners, be crucified, and three days later rise to life.' "*

And in Matthew 28:5-10, *"The Angel spoke to the women. 'You must not be afraid,' he said, 'I know you are looking for Jesus, who was crucified. He is not here; he has been raised, just as he said. Come here and see the place where he was lying.' Go quickly now, and tell his disciples, He has been raised from death, and now he is going to Galilee*

ahead of you; there you will see him!' Remember
what I have told you. So they left the tomb in a
hurry, afraid and yet filled with joy, and ran to
tell his disciples. Suddenly Jesus met them and
said, 'Peace be with you.' They came up to him,
took hold of his feet, and worshipped him. 'Do not
be afraid,' Jesus said to them. 'Go and tell my
brothers to go to Galilee, and there they will see
me."

We know that Jesus did rise from the dead
because the disciples who saw Him were willing
to die as martyrs. The modern Church would
not exist if Jesus was not alive in our hearts.
There are still many martyrs around the world
in our day, which prefer death to having to deny
their belief in Jesus.

Today, many miracles are done in the name of
Jesus every day and in every country.

The Jews expected the Messiah to save them
from the Roman oppression, but that would have
been temporal. God had a bigger plan and that
was to offer his Son as a sacrifice for Man's sins
and to last for eternity as the Bible says in
John 3:16-17, *"For God loved the world so much*
that he gave his only Son, so that everyone who
believes in him may not die, but have eternal life.
For God did not send his Son into the world to be
its judge, but to be its Saviour."

The Jews were driven out of the city by the Roman legions from 68 to 73 A.D. Many of the Jews were killed and the survivors were sent to work as slaves throughout the Roman Empire. These events were foretold in the Bible in Luke 19:43-44, *"The time will come when your enemies will surround you with barricades, blockade you, and close in on you from every side. They will completely destroy you and the people within your walls, not a single stone will they leave in its place, because you did not recognize the time when God came to save you.* This is recorded again in Luke 21:24, *"Some will be killed by the sword, and others will be taken as prisoners to all countries; and the heathen will trample over Jerusalem until their time is up."*

What happened to the Jews in exile? In the following chapters here is what my research has come up with.

I want to thank **Google, the Jewish Virtual Library, and Wikipedia** for making the research so easy.

Chapter 7

In History there are many examples of

EXPULSIONS OF THE JEWS

France	1182
England	1290
Spain	1492
Portugal	1493

FROM FRANCE

The Jews had already been settled in France for over a thousand years when Philip Augustus became King in 1179. This brilliant but unscrupulous ruler, then about fifteen years of age, needed money to strengthen his hold on the throne and to fight the powerful feudal barons. He gained these objectives, in part, by confiscating Jewish wealth.

Four months after taking over the reigns of government he imprisoned all the Jews in his lands and released them only after a heavy ransom had been paid (1180). The next year (1181) he annulled all loans made to Christians by Jews, taking instead a comfortable twenty per cent for himself. A year later (1182) he confiscated all the lands and buildings of the Jews and drove them out of the lands governed by himself directly.

RESULT : The king had an unhappy family life. After the early death in childbirth of his first wife Isabelle in 1190, Philip decided to marry again. He married Ingeborg of Denmark. However, Philip was repelled by her, refused to allow her to be crowned Queen and confine her to a convent.

Philip sought a new bride and wanted to marry Margherite of Geneva, but Thomas I of Savoy kidnapped her and married her instead. Philip then married Agnes of Merania and had 2 children. Pope Innocent III declared Philip's 3rd marriage null and void and placed France under an interdict in 1199. Philip was finally forced to have Ingeborg back as his Queen in 1213.

"I will curse those who curse you."

Is this just a coincidence?

FROM ENGLAND

The first Jewish communities of significant size came to England with William the Conqueror in 1066. The Jews were declared to be direct subjects of the King, unlike the rest of the population. This had advantages for Jews, in that they were not tied to any particular lord, but were subject to the whims of the king. Every successive King formally reviewed a royal charter granting Jews the right to remain in England. Jews did not enjoy any of the guarantees of the Magna Carta of 1215.

Economically, Jews played a key role in the country. The church at the time strictly forbade the lending of money for profit. This instruction did not apply to the Jews as a consequence, some Jews made large amounts of money. As the Jews were his subjects, the King levied very heavy taxes on them without having to summon Parliament for their approval on the taxes he proposed.

The Jews acquired a reputation as extortionate money lenders which made them extremely unpopular with both the Church and the general public. Anti-Semitism was widespread culminating in 1190 when over a hundred Jews were murdered. The situation continued to get worse for the Jews and in 1217, England became the first European nation to require the Jews to wear a form of identification and the King continued to issue heavier levies year by year. The rising influence of Italian bankers made Jewish financial services superfluous by 1265 and the Jewish rights were gradually restricted.

In those days Royalty married each other. Edward of England married Eleanor of Castile (Spain) when he was 15 and she was 13 in 1254. They had 16 children and she went with him every where including one of the Crusades. His father, King Henry III, died when he was in the 9th Crusade so Edward came back to England and was crowned on the 19th August, 1274.

In 1275 Edward I signed the Statute of Jewry outlawing all lending of money for profit and gave the Jews 15 years to readjust. Local prejudice made Jewish movement into mercantile or agricultural areas impossible. The Jews eventually were all expelled from England by an edict signed by Edward I on the 18th July, 1290. About 16,000 Jews had to leave England by All Saint's Day (1st November, 1290). All their property was seized by the crown and all outstanding debts payable to Jews were transferred to the King's name.

RESULT : The death of Eleanor in Nottinghamshire on the 28th November, 1290 affected Edward deeply. We know that Edward loved Eleanor because he displayed his grief by erecting 12 very expensive and elaborate crosses where her coffin stopped each night on its way to London. (The Eleanor crosses were built between 1291 to 1294 in Lincoln, Grantham, Stamford, Stony Stratford, Woburn, Dunstable,

St. Alban, Cheapside, and Charing Cross. Only 3 crosses are still standing in Waltham Cross, Northampton and Geddington.)

His heir failed to develop the expected kingly character, and Edward also failed in his dearest wish to conquer Scotland.

"I will curse those who curse you."

Is this just a coincidence?

FROM SPAIN

In 1469 Ferdinand and Isabella married bringing together the principal kingdoms of Spain: Aragon and Castile which led to the unification of Spain.

When the overt hostility against the Jews became more pronounced in brutal episodes of violence and oppression, thousands of Jews converted to Catholicism. At first these conversions seemed an effective solution to the cultural conflict, but their success made these New Christians unpopular with the church and royal hierarchies. These suspicions on the part of Catholics were only heightened by the fact that some of the coerced conversions were undoubtedly insincere. They embrace Christianity, while privately adhering to their Jewish practice and faith. These secret practitioners are commonly referred to as marranos. Ferdinand and Isabella took seriously the reports that some marranos were not only privately practicing their former faith, but were secretly trying to draw back into the Jewish fold. In 1480, the king and queen created the Spanish Inquisition to investigate these suspicions; in the next 12 years thousands of converted Jews were killed.

In 1492 the surrender of the city of Granada placed yet another large Jewish population under their rule so on the 31st March, 1492 Ferdinand II of Aragon and Isabella of Castile signed the Alhambra Decree ordering the expulsion of all Jews from the Kingdom of Spain and its territories and possessions by 31st July 1492. The King did not allow them to carry silver and gold out of his country, so that they were compelled to exchange their silver and gold for merchandise of cloths and skins and other things.

RESULT : Isabella's plan for her children did not work out. Their eldest son, Juan died shortly after his marriage. Isabella, Princess of Asturias died in childbirth and her son Miguel died at the age of two. Isabella's, titles passed to her daughter, Joan the crazy.

"I will curse those who curse you."

Is this just a coincidence?

FROM PORTUGAL

After the Jew's expulsion from Spain 120,000 Spanish Jews went to Portugal paying one ducat each and one fourth of the value of their merchandise to King John II of Portugal. He only allowed them to stay in his country for 6 months. This King acted far worse towards them than the King of Spain: He banished 700 children to St. Thomas, a remote island off the coast of Africa where all of them died. Upon them the Scriptural word was fulfilled if they did evil and rejected the Lord, Deuteronomy 28:32, *"Yours sons and your daughters will be given as slaves to foreigners while you look on. Every day you will strain your eyes for your children to return."* He made slaves of all the Jews who remained in Portugal in 1493.

RESULT : John II had no male heir when he died, was not popular during his reign as he was known as a tyrant. (He was succeeded by his first cousin: Manuel).

"I will curse those who curse you."

Is this just a coincidence?

Chapter 8

COUNTRIES

Can countries be blessed or cursed in relation to how they treat Israel? Let us look into history:

BRITISH EMPIRE

The British Empire was the largest empire in history. A common saying at the time was "The sun did not set on the British Empire" because they had countries all over the world so the sun was always shining on at least one of them.

After the allies won World War I and the collapse of the Ottoman Empire, the British Government was given a Mandate for the land of Palestine. The borders of this land extended from the Mediterranean Sea to the west, Mesopotamia to the east, Lebanon to the north, Syria to the northeast, Saudi Arabia to the south east and Egypt to the southwest.

The British Cabinet had a meeting on 31st October, 1917 and agreed that the British government supported a Jewish "national home" in Palestine. Therefore on the 2nd November the Foreign Secretary, Arthur James Balfour wrote a letter to Lord Rothschild, which is called the **Balfour Declaration** : 2nd November, 1917:

Dear Lord Rothschild, I have much pleasure in conveying to you, on behalf of His Majesty's Government, the following declaration of sympathy with Jewish Zionist aspirations which has been submitted to, and approved by, the Cabinet: "His Majesty's Government view with favour the establishment in Palestine of a national home for the Jewish people, and will use their best endeavours to facilitate the achievement of this object, it being clearly understood that nothing shall be done which may prejudice the civil and religious rights of existing non-Jewish communities in Palestine, or the rights and political status enjoyed by Jews in any other country". I should be grateful if you would bring this declaration to the knowledge of the Zionist Federation.

Yours sincerely,

Arthur James Balfour

The Balfour Declaration was later incorporated into the Sèvres peace treaty with Turkey.

RESULT : The British Empire flourished.

"I will bless those who bless you."

Is this just a coincidence?

In 1921, the British Empire ruled over a population of about 458 million people, approximately one-quarter of the world's population and ruled over a quarter of the total land area of the world.

Unfortunately in 1921 Winston Churchill as Colonial Secretary signed away 77% of the land promised to the Jews in the Balfour declaration and formed the Trans Jordan territory not keeping the promise made to form the state of Israel.

In September 1922, the British government presented a memorandum to the League of Nations stating that Transjordan would be excluded from all the provisions dealing with Jewish settlement, and this memorandum was approved on 23 September. From that point onwards, Britain administered the part west of the Jordan, 23% of the entire territory as "Palestine", and the part east of the Jordan, 77% of the entire territory, as "Transjordan." Technically they remained one mandate but most official documents referred to them as if they were two separate mandates. Transfer of authority to an Arab government took place gradually in Transjordan, starting with the recognition of a local administration in 1923 and transfer of most administrative functions in 1928.

RESULT : 77% percent of the land of the British

Empire now has been lost by the countries becoming independent.

"I will curse those who curse you."

Is this just a coincidence?

The White Paper of 1939, which placed immigration restrictions on Jews going into Palestine, stated that the Jewish population "has risen to some 450,000" and was "approaching a third of the entire population of the country". In 1945, a demographic study showed that the population had grown to 1,764,520, comprising 1,061,270 Muslims, 553,600 Jews, 135,550 Christians and 14,100 people of other groups.

Britain continued to rule over the 23% of Palestine with a pro-Arab administration. During the war, the British forbade entry into Palestine of European Jews escaping Nazi persecution, placing them in detention camps or deporting them to places such a Mauritius.

They kept the immigration quotas very strict and after the holocaust when 6 million Jews died, and ships came full of Jews from Europe, the British would send the ships back. They also made interment camps in Cyprus keeping them away from Israel. They supplied arms to the Arabs, but arrested any Israelite with weapons.

At the UN, when countries voted whether they wanted the formation of Israel, Britain abstained.

RESULT : Britain lost rule over the following countries:

1947 : India, Canada

1948 : Mandate of Palestine, Ceylon, Burma

1957 : Malaya, Ghana

1960 : Nigeria, Somaliland

1961 : Sierra Leone, Union of South Africa

1962 : Uganda, Jamaica, Trinidad and Tobago

1963 : Kenya and Zanzibar

1964 : Tanganyika, Zambia (Northern Rhodesia), Malta, Gozo, Belize (British Honduras)

1965 : The Gambia

1966 : Lesotho (Basutoland), Barbados, Guyana

1967 : Botswana (Bechuanaland)

1968 : Swaziland

1981 : Antigua and Barbuda

1997 : Hong Kong – the United Kingdom's last major overseas territory.

The Suez Crisis in 1956 marked a turning point in the history of Britain and its empire, demonstrating Britain's decline as a world power, unable to act alone, for it was now dependent on the support of the United States.

The United Kingdom retains sovereignty over Gibraltar, the Falkland Islands and the British Antarctic Territory. These territories are being claimed by Spain, Argentina and Chile respectively. Most former British colonies are members of the Commonwealth of Nations, a non-political, voluntary Association of equal members, in which the United Kingdom has no privileged status.

"I will curse those who curse you."

Is this just a coincidence?

INDIA

The British Empire lost its most valuable colony when the British Raj came to an end in August 1947 due to a 50 year continuous campaign for independence. Because of the religious differences, India was partitioned into two countries: India (mostly Hindu) and Pakistan (mostly Muslim).

In November 1947 when India was asked in the UN to vote for the formation of the country of Israel, they voted against. India's view was that the state of Israel was an imperialist creation, a state whose basis for creation was similar to the formation of Pakistan: religion.

India followed this policy for decades backing the Palestinian struggle. They also needed the Arab oil and support of Muslim countries in their fight over Kashmir with Pakistan.

RESULT : During 1947 and until the cease fire in January 1949, thousands of people died when huge riots broke out when Muslims and Hindus began to flee into their preferred countries. The Kashmir issue has not been resolved and India and Pakistan went to war again in 1965 and 1999.

"I will curse those who curse you."

Is this just a coincidence?

India began to revise its Israel policy at the end of the cold war in 1990 and after the Gulf War in 1991, so in 1992 India established full diplomatic ties with Israel.

RESULT : Looking at the prosperity and development of India it can be seen that after 1992, India really progressed and prospered.

In 1998, when India tested its nuclear weapons, Israel was among the few countries that did not condemn it.

"I will bless those who bless you."

Is this just a coincidence?

RUSSIA

When Alexander II was murdered in 1881, a new period of anti-Jewish discrimination and severe persecution began and lasted for a century.

In 1891 the Jews are expelled from Moscow and when in 1905 Russia lost the war with Japan, the Jews were blamed. The Black Hundreds openly declared their plan to exterminate the Jews.

The fall of the Czar in March 1917 initially brought great freedom to the Jews in Russia: Synagogues and schools were opened and life flourished, but this freedom was short lived as in November 1917 Lenin declared "the slogan of the rabbis and the bourgeois is the slogan of our enemies."

The ensuing Civil War turned the Ukraine into a battlefield. In 1919 the army's slogan is "Strike at the Jews and save Russia." At the end of the Civil War an estimated 100,000 Jews were dead and more than a half a million homeless. The Hebrew language was the only language outlawed.

When the United Nations voted on the formation of Israel in 1948 Russia voted in favour, but this was mainly in opposition to "British Imperialist Policy". Soon afterwards Russia adopted a friendly policy towards the Middle East Arab countries to the detriment of Israel.

During the Stalinist purges million of Jews were killed or sent to brutal labour camps where thousands of Jews were exiled to Siberia. The pressure all over Russia was for Jews to forego their identity so their Hebrew language was outlawed and also their means of livelihood. This eradication of all traces of the Jews lasted until 1953 when Stalin died. Over 70 years, the Jews were reduced from 5 million to less than half a million.

RESULT : *Russia lost its Empire :* Armenia, Azerbaijan, Belarus, Georgia, Kazakhstan, Kyrgyzstan, Latvia, Lithuania, Moldova, Tajikistan, Turkmenistan, Ukraine and Uzbekistan are now independent.

"I will curse those who curse you."

Is this just a coincidence?

GERMANY

In the 1930s, plans to isolate and eventually eliminate Jews completely in Germany began with the construction of ghettos, concentration camps, and labour camps. In 1933 the Dachau concentration camp was built.

In 1935 the Nuremberg Laws were passed, stripping Jews of their German citizenship and denied government employment. Most Jews employed by Germans lost their jobs at this time, which were being taken by unemployed Germans. The Nazi government attempted to send 17,000 German Jews of Polish descent back to Poland, a decision which led to the assassination of Ernst vom Rath by Herschel Grynszpan, a German Jew living in France. This provided the pretext for a pogrom the Nazi Party incited against the Jews on 9th November, 1938, which specifically targeted Jewish businesses. The event was called Kristallnacht (Night of Broken Glass). In one night 1,574 Jewish Synagogues were burnt to the ground; over 1,300 Jews were killed; 30,000 Jews were arrested and sent to concentration camps; 7,000 Jewish businesses were destroyed and thousand of Jewish homes were ransacked. By September 1939, more than 200,000 Jews had left Germany, with the Nazi government seizing any property they left behind.

Using Darwin's theory of survival of the fittest, the Nazis killed tens of thousands of disabled and sick Germans in an effort to "maintain the purity of the German Master race" Under a law passed in 1933, the Nazi regime carried out the compulsory sterilization of over 400,000 individuals labeled as having hereditary defects. The techniques of mass killing developed in these

51

efforts would later be used in the Holocaust to get rid of the Jews.

At the outset of World War II, the German authority in occupied Poland ordered that all Jews face compulsory labour and that those who were physically incapable such as women and children were to be confined to ghettos.

In 1942, at the Wannsee Conference, Nazi officials decided to eliminate the Jews altogether, as the "Final Solution of the Jewish Question". Concentration camps like Auschwitz were converted into gas chambers to kill as many Jews as possible.

When Germany took control of countries such as Poland, the Nazy party decided to eliminate all the Jews and started shooting them and burying them in mass graves. They then decided to send all the remaining Jews in trains to six extermination camps named Auschwitz, Belzec, Chelmno, Lublin-Majdanek, Sobibor and Treblinka.

By 1945, six concentration camps had been liberated by Allied forces and they found the few survivors to be severely malnourished. The Allies also found evidence that the Nazis were profiteering from the mass murder of Jews not only by confiscating their property and personal valuables but also by extracting gold teeth fillings from the dead bodies.

RESULT : Germany lost the war and was impoverished for many years.

"I will curse those who curse you."

Is this just a coincidence?

Subsequently, since World War II, Germany, in an act of national contrition has made many money contributions to Israel for their part in the holocaust. It is an irony of history that the country the Nazi Party wanted to purge of Jews now has the fastest growing Jewish community in Western Europe. Before the Nazi's came to power, about 600,000 Jews lived in Germany. Between 1945 and 1952 some 200,000 Jewish displaced persons lived in disused concentration camps and urban centres in Germany. Most of them immigrated to Israel when the state was created. By the time the Berlin Wall fell, Germany's Jews were only 30,000. In 1991 German had a law which granted Jews special refugee status. Between 1991 and 2005, more than 200,000 Jews from the former Soviet Union immigrated to Germany.

Germany's growing prosperity and its readiness to come to terms with its Nazi past encouraged Jews to settle in Germany. The city of Berlin give the Jewish community a yearly budget of 25 million Euros to maintain the Synagogues, schools, cemeteries, library, hospitals and nursing homes as an atonement for the past. Germany now has 89 Synagogues. Hundreds of memorials now dot Germany from concentration camp museums to brass bricks sunk in the pavement outside ordinary houses naming the Jews who once lived there. A Holocaust Memorial was built in the heart of the city of Berlin. There is also the Topography of Terror, which is an entire block in the city centre, which once housed the headquarters of the Reich security services. In May 2005, the new Holocaust Memorial was inaugurated. It is an undulating labyrinth of 2,711 concrete blocks on a site the size of a football field near the Brandenburg Gate. A Jewish Museum opened in Munich in March, 2007 and a new glass covered courtyard opened in Berlin inspired by the sharpness and angles of barbed wire.

On the 17th March, 2008 Angela Merkel, the German Chancellor, visited Israel and pledged unwavering support for Israel in an address to the Israel Parliament aimed at cementing ties with the Jewish state after its creation following the Nazi Holocaust.

RESULT : Germany is prospering.

"I will bless those who bless you."

Is this just a coincidence?

REPUBLIC OF IRELAND

The history of the Jews in Ireland extends back nearly a thousand years and they have been well-accepted into Irish life.

Ireland's first Synagogue was founded in 1660 near Dublin Castle, and the first Jewish cemetery was founded in the early eighteenth century. In 1746 a bill was introduced in the Irish House of Commons "for naturalizing persons professing the Jewish religion in Ireland". The Irish Marriage Act of 1844 expressly made provision for marriages according to Jewish rites.

Daniel O'Connell is best known for the campaign for Catholic Emancipation; he also supported similar efforts for Jews. In 1846, at his insistence, the British law "De Judaismo", which prescribed a special dress for Jews, was repealed. O'Connell said: "Ireland has claims on your ancient race, it is the only country that I know of unsullied by any one act of persecution of the Jews".

During the great famine of the 1840s, many Jews gave generously towards Famine relief. Ireland's Jews were city folk, business people, professionals, merchants who bought their food instead of growing it.

In 1966, the Dublin Jewish community arranged the planting and dedication of the Éamon de

Valera Forest in Israel, near Nazareth in recognition of his consistent support for Ireland's Jews.

RESULT : Ireland is one of the richest, most developed and peaceful countries on earth, having the fifth highest Gross Domestic Product per capita, second highest Gross Domestic Product (Purchasing Power Parity) per capita and having the fifth highest Human Development Index rank.

The Republic of Ireland also boasts the highest quality of life in the world, ranking first in the Economist Intelligence Unit's Quality of life index. Ireland was ranked fourth on the Global Peace Index. Ireland also has high rankings for its education system, political freedom and civil rights, press freedom and economic freedom.

"I will bless those who bless you."

Is this just a coincidence?

OTHER COUNTRIES

Eleven of the 13 countries that voted against the State of Israel on 29th November, 1947 are:

Afghanistan, Syria, Iran , Iraq, Lebanon, Pakistan, Saudi Arabia, Yemen, Cuba, Egypt, and Greece.

RESULT : The countries have been in constant strife.

"I will curse those who curse you."

Is this just a coincidence?

Although Turkey and India were among the countries that voted against the State of Israel, they are now two of Israel's closest allies.

RESULT : Turkey and India are becoming prosperous.

"I will bless those who bless you."

Is this just a coincidence?

Chapter 9

PEOPLE

Do God's words about blessing and cursing with regard to Israel also pertain to individual people? Yes. Very clearly, and this can be seen by the lives of the following people:

WINSTON CHURCHILL

I often wondered why the British people did not award Winston Churchill with grateful thanks for winning the war by electing him as Prime Minister in his own right, but he was under a curse. How did this happen?

When David Lloyd George was Prime Minister, he appointed Winston Churchill as Colonial Secretary. In 1921 Winston Churchill was persuaded by T.E. Lawrence (known as Lawrence of Arabia) to assign 77% of the land promised to be the Jewish National Home to be the Transjordan territory. Winston Churchill disregarded the consensus among British ministers that the boundary between Palestine and the Arab state should run ten miles east of the River Jordan. It is obvious he was not au fait with the words of the Bible either about Abraham and his descendants: Genesis 12 verse 3, *"I will bless those who bless you, but I will curse those who curse you. And through you I will bless all the nations.*

RESULT : Winston Churchill lost his seat in the 1922 General Election. He was also humiliated by not being elected Prime Minister immediately after winning World War II when Atlee won victory by a land slide.

"I will curse those who curse you."

Is this just a coincidence?

DAVID LLOYD GEORGE

When David Lloyd George was Prime Minister, the land of Israel was given away when the formation of the Trans Jordan territory was signed in 1921 in contradiction to which had been understood as the borders of the Jewish National Home at the time of the Balfour Declaration.

RESULT : On the 12th October 1922, he was brought down by the Conservatives ending the coalition. He was defeated in the subsequent election and throughout the next two decades Lloyd George remained on the margins of British politics, being frequently predicted to return to office, but never succeeding.

"I will curse those who curse you."

Is this just a coincidence?

LAWRENCE OF ARABIA

Immediately after the First World War, Lawrence worked for the Foreign Office, attending the Paris Peace Conference as a member of Faisal's delegation.

In 1921 he served as an advisor to Winston Churchill at the Colonial Office. It was through his influence saying that Britain was indebted to Emir Faisal that Winston Churchill gave 77% of the land that was promised to be the State of Israel to create the territory of Trans Jordan.

RESULT : From 1921, his life went downhill: not happy in his job, he attempted to join the Royal Air Force under the name of John Hume Ross, but he was exposed and thrown out. He changed his name to T.E. Shaw and joined the Royal Tank Corps in 1923, he was unhappy there and repeatedly petitioned to rejoin the RAF, which finally admitted him in August 1925. He was moved to a remote base in British India and remained until 1928 when he was forced to return to the UK after rumours began to circulate that he was involved in espionage activities.

He was not happy with his finances either as he purchased a plot of land in Chingford and built a hut and swimming pool there. This was demolished in 1930 when the City of London

Corporation acquired the land. He died in a motor cycle accident in Dorset and people erroneously believe that he was given the honour of being buried in St. Paul's Cathedral. He is buried in the family plot of his cousins, the Framptons in the village of Moreton in Dorset.

"I will curse those who curse you."

Is this just a coincidence?

ANTHONY EDEN

When Anthony Eden was British Foreign Secretary in World War II, he was strongly opposed to the State of Israel in 1944.

RESULT : Eden's eldest son, Simon Eden, while serving as a pilot with the RAF in Burma in the latter days of the Second World War, went missing in action, later declared dead, There was a close bond between Anthony and Simon Eden : His son's death was a great personal shock to him and he became even more depressed when his first marriage broke up.

During an operation in 1953 to remove his gallstones, the surgeon damaged his bile duct. This blunder made Eden vulnerable to recurrent infections and attacks of violent pain and fevers. To overcome this weakness Eden was prescribed the wonder drug of the 1950s – Benzedrine regarded by doctors in the 1950s as a harmless stimulant. This illegal drug we now call speed! It has been suggested that Eden's medication affected his mood and decision during the subsequent Suez crisis. He is mainly remembered for his role in the Suez Crisis of 1956, which was politically disastrous from a British perspective and Eden is ranked among the least successful British Prime Ministers of the 20th century.

"I will curse those who curse you."

Is this just a coincidence?

HITLER

Hitler was the leader of the Nazi Party, which pursued its racial policy aims through persecution and killing of those considered "impure" or otherwise "enemies of the Reich." Especially targeted were minority groups such as the Jews, Gypsies, black people and people with mental or physical disabilities.

Martin Luther wrote a treatise called "Von den Jüden und ihren Lügen" (On the Jews and Their Lies) in 1543 in which he says that the Jew's homes should be destroyed, their synagogues burnt, money confiscated, their liberty curtailed and even advocating murdering them.

(This is totally against the teachings of Jesus who advocates love towards every one including ones enemies. Murder is a sin against the 10 Commandments.)

400 Years later, Hitler used these words by Martin Luther as an excuse to exterminate the Jews and as a result he killed 6 millions Jews.

RESULT : Hitler committed suicide when he knew he could not win the war. The Third Reich was meant to last one thousand years, but did not even last 11 years!

"I will curse those who curse you."

Is this just a coincidence?

IDI AMIN

Idi Amin joined the British colonial regiment, the King's African Rifles, in 1946. He advanced to the rank of Major General and Commander of the Ugandan Army.

He deposed Milton Obote in a military coup in 1971 and said that he was a soldier, not a politician and that the military government would remain only as a caretaker regime until new elections could be held. Idi Amin was initially welcomed both within Uganda and by the international community as he had freed many political prisoners, and reiterated his promise to hold free and fair elections to return the country to democratic rule in the shortest period possible.

One week after the coup, Amin declared himself President of Uganda, Commander in Chief of the armed forces, Army Chief of Staff and Chief of Air Staff. He suspended certain provisions of the constitution and placed military tribunals above the system of civil law. He replaced the General Service Unit an intelligence agency by the State Research Bureau. The headquarters of the SRB became the scene of torture and executions over the next several years.

Idi Amin, expelled the Jewish military advisers, and persecuted the Jews by outlawing Jewish rituals and destroying the Jewish Synagogues.

Then on 27th June 1976, an Air France Airbus A300, which was flying from Tel Aviv to Paris via Athens, was hijacked soon after taking off from Athens. The plane was hijacked by two Palestinians belonging to the Popular Front for the Liberation of Palestine – External Operations and two members of the German Revolutionary movement. On board were 246 passengers and 12 crew. The plane was diverted to Libya where it stayed on the ground for 7 hours to refuel. One female hostage, who was pregnant, was released.

As Uganda's President, Idi Amin was sympathetic to the Palestinian cause, the aircraft flew to Entebbe Airport in Uganda where three additional terrorists joined the hijackers and Uganda's military forces were deployed effectively in support of the terrorists.

The terrorists demanded the release of 40 Palestinian prisoners held by Israel, as well as others held in France, Germany, Switzerland and Kenya. They threatened to begin killing hostages on lst July if their demands were not met. In the meantime, the terrorists held the hostages in the transit hall at Entebbe Airport. 156 hostages who did not hold Israeli passports were released and flown to safety, while 83 Jews and Israeli citizens, as well as 20 others who refused to abandon them, continued to be held hostage.

Soon after the hijacking, the Israeli military began preparing for a possible rescue operation. It was clear that such a rescue mission would be extremely challenging, because of the great distances involved and the large number of hostages. The Israeli rescue operation freed all the hostages; although 3 of them died and 10 were wounded. 1 Israeli solider, 45 Uganda soldiers and 6 hijackers were killed. The raid is generally considered a great anti-terrorist success, especially in view of the tremendous logistical challenges which had been overcome, and the low casualties among both the hostages and commandos.

At the time of the raid, one hostage, Dora Bloch, a 75-year old woman, was not present at the airport. She had been taken to Mulago hospital in Kampala, following a choking incident. Dora Bloch was subsequently murdered on Idi Amin's orders

RESULT : Idi Amin was overthrown in 1979, when he lost the war Between Uganda and Tanzania.

"I will curse those who curse you."

Is this just a coincidence?

Is there an example in the last Century of blessings and curses with regards to the Jews?

ALEXANDER III

In 1894 Alexander III of Russia expelled all the Jews from Yalta.

RESULT : During a holiday in Yalta, some weeks after ordering the expulsion of the Jews, he died.

"I will curse those who curse you."

Is this just a coincidence?

Chapter 10

STATE OF ISRAEL

The Bible predicted the day when Israel would be a Nation again[1]

Ezekiel 4:1 *"God said, "Mortal man, get a brick, put it in front of you, and scratch lines on it to represent the city of Jerusalem. Then to represent a siege, put trenches, earthworks, camps, and battering rams all round it. Take an iron pan and set it up like a wall between you and the city. Face the city. It is under siege, and you are the one besieging it. This will be a sign to the nation of Israel.* **"Then lie down on your left side, and I will place on you the guilt of the nation of Israel. For 390 days you will stay there and suffer because of their guilt. I have sentenced you to one day for each year** *their punishment* **will last. When you finish that turn over on your right side and suffer for the guilt of Judah for 40 days – one day for each year** *of their punishment."*

```
    390 days (on the left side)
 +   40  days (on the right side)
    430 days = 430 years
 –   70 years  paid in exile in Babylon
    360 years
```

Leviticus 26:23-24, **"If after all this punishment you still do not listen to me, but continue to defy** *me, then I will turn on you and punish you 7 times harder than before."*

        360 years
    x 7 years
    2,520 years which have to be paid in exile
    x 360 Biblical year has 360 days
    907,200 Biblical days that have to be paid in exile

The Gregorian Calendar has 365 1/4 days so divide 907,200 by 365. 25 to get the actual year = 2,483.8

According to our Gregorian Calendar the Jews returned from their exile in Babylon in the spring of 536.

        2483.8

    – 536.3 (Day that they came back from Babylon.)

        1947.5 (Year 1 is the beginning of the year)
    + 1

    1948.5

MAY 1948

A vote was taken in the UN. It was passed by 33 votes to 13, with 10 abstentions, creating the final push for the creation of the State of Israel.

Making the words in the Bible come true:

Amos 9:11, *The Lord says, "A day is coming when I will restore the kingdom of David, which is like a house fallen into ruins. I will repair its walls and restore it. I will rebuild it and make it as it was long ago."*

Israel became a nation in a day on 14th May, 1948 !

Although Israel was born in a day, the Jews had to fight hard from the beginning to keep the territory, as the Secretary General of the League of Arab States sent an official cablegram on the 15th May, 1948 stating publicly, their intention of creating a "United State of Palestine" in place of the Jewish and Arab, two-state, UN Plan. They claimed the latter was invalid, as it was opposed by Palestine's Arab majority, and maintained that the absence of legal authority made it necessary to intervene to protect Arab lives and property.

At the beginning of 1948 Amin al-Husayni was in exile in Egypt. He was the Grand Mufti of Jerusalem, who during the second half of World War II, was in Germany making radio broadcasts exhorting Muslims to ally with the Nazis in the war against their common enemy: the Jews. In one of these broadcasts, he said, "Arabs, arise as one man and fight for your sacred rights. Kill

Jews wherever you find them. This pleases God, history, and religion. This saves your honor. God is with you." In the immediate aftermath of the Holocaust, such statements by Arab leaders (along with the Mufti's violently anti-Semitic history) led to a widespread belief that the Israelis were facing a new genocide.

The Transjordanian troops entered Jerusalem two days after Independence, and heavy house to house fighting occurred expelling all the Jews living in the Jewish Quarter and destroying the main Synagogue in Jerusalem.

Israel, the United States and the Soviets called the Arab states' entry into Palestine illegal aggression, while UN secretary general Trygve Lie characterized it as "the first armed aggression which the world had seen since the end of the Second World War"

On paper, the new nation of Israel did not stand a chance fighting against 7 oil rich Arab countries, who did not have to travel too far, but Israel had God on their side.

Amos 9:15, "I will plant my people on the land I gave them, and they will not be pulled up again. The Lord your God has spoken"

This is what happened : The day that Israel declared its independence was the start of the second phase of the 1948 Palestinian war with several Arab armies entering Israel. The Arab Legion had about 10,000 soldiers which were trained and commanded by British officers. King Abdullah I of Jordan became supreme commander of the Arab forces. The table below shows the strength on both sides:

Strength Israel	Strength of Arab Countries
Initially 29,677	Egypt 10,000 initially, rising to 20,000
4th June 40,285	Iraq 5,000 initially, rising to 15,000 – 18,000
17th July 63,586	Syria 2,500 – 5,000
7th October 88,033	Transjordan 6,000 – 12,000
28th October 92,275	Lebanon 1,000 initially, rising to 2,000
2nd December 106,900	Saudi Arabia 800 – 1,200
23rd December 107,652	Yemen – unknown
30th December 108,300	Arab Liberation Army 3,500 – 6,000

Usually when a country is fighting 7 other countries, there is no immigration. Israel was different: people who came thought it was worthwhile to come to Israel even if it meant dying for their new country. An average of 10,300 immigrants came each month and many of the immigrants died.

The Israeli Air Force purchased 25 Avia S-199 planes from Czechoslovakia. This created the ironic situation of the young Jewish state using German-designed planes to help counter the British-designed Spitfires flown by Egypt. The Israel Air Force achieved air superiority by the fall of 1948.

The first mission of the Israeli Defense Force was to hold on against the Arab armies and stop them from destroying major Jewish settlements, until reinforcements and weapons arrived.

In the north, the Syrian army was blocked in the kibbutz Degania, where the settlers managed to stop the Syrian armored forces with only light weapons. One tank that was disabled by a Molotov cocktail is still present at the kibbutz. Later, an artillery bombardment, made by cannons jury-rigged from 19th century museum pieces, led to the withdrawal of the Syrians from the kibbutz. (Bringing memories of David and Goliath.)

RESULT : Decisive Israeli victory, tactical and strategic Arab failure. The 1949 Armistice Agreement: The State of Israel retained nearly all the territory that had been assigned to it in the 1947 UN Partition Plan, as well as conquering half of the land intended to become the Arab state of Palestine and a portion of the territory intended for international administration around Jerusalem;

for international administration around Jerusalem; Transjordan occupied the West Bank and Egypt occupied the Gaza Strip.

"I will bless those who bless you."

Is this just a coincidence?

This was the first in a series of wars fought between Israel and its Arab neighbors. The Palestinian Liberation Organization formed in 1964 was a terrorist organization bent on Israel's annihilation. Palestinian rioting, demonstrations, and terrorist acts against Israelis became chronic.

Chapter 11

6 – DAY WAR

In reaction to mounting Israeli-Syrian tensions in 1967, Egypt amassed 1,000 tanks and 100,000 soldiers on the border, closed the Straits of Tiran to all ships flying Israeli Flags or carrying strategic materials, and called for unified Arab action against Israel. In response, on June 5th, Israel launched a pre-emptive attack against Egypt's air force. Jordan, which had signed a mutual defense treaty with Egypt, then attacked western Jerusalem.

Again, Israel was outnumbered in everything mortal, but again God was on their side otherwise how could they have won?

Here is a comparison of their strength:

Strength of Israel	Strength of Arab Countries
Israel 264,000	Egypt 240,000, Syria, Jordan, Lebanon and Iraq 307,000
300 combat aircraft	957 combat aircraft
800 tanks	2,504 tanks

RESULT : Israel was able to expand their territory by capturing the Gaza Strip and the Sinai Peninsula all the way up to the Suez Canal from Egypt, the West Bank (including East Jerusalem) from Jordan, and half of the Golan Heights from Syria in just 6 days!

The Jews took control of the whole of Jerusalem on June 7, 1967, and celebrated the reunification of their capital by Rabbi Shlomo Gorens sounding a shofar at the Western Wall.

Another war won under impossible odds making the words of the Bible come true once again: Amos 9:15, *I will plant my people on the land I gave them, and they will not be pulled up again. The Lord your God has spoken"*

"I will bless those who bless you."

Is this just a coincidence?

Chapter 12

YOM KIPPUR WAR

The Yom Kippur War was fought from 6th October to 26th October, 1973 by a coalition of Arab states led by Egypt and Syria against Israel. The war began with a surprise joint attack by Egypt and Syria on the Jewish holiday of Yom Kippur.

Yom Kippur (the Day of Atonement), is one of the holidays of the Bible as it says in Lev. 23:27-28, *"The tenth day of the seventh month is the day when the annual ritual is to be performed to take away the sins of the people. On that day do not eat anything at all; come together for worship, and present a food offering to the Lord. Do not work on that day, because it is the day for performing the ritual to take away sin."* Jews have traditionally observed this holiday with a 25-hour period of fasting and intensive prayer.

Egypt and Syria crossed the cease-fire lines in the Sinai and Golan Heights, respectively, which had been captured by Israel in 1967 during the 6-Day War. The Egyptians and Syrians advanced during the first 24 – 48 hours.

This was the comparison of their strength and again on paper the Arabs should have won:

Strength of Israel	Strength of Arab countries
415,000 troops	1,000,000 troops
1,500 tanks	63,800 tanks
3,000 armored carriers	3,700 armored carriers
945 artillery units	1,920 artillery units
561 planes	799 planes
84 helicopters	182 helicopters
38 Navy vessels	125 Navy vessels

But God proved again that he was blessing Israel and even though they were really outnumbered, they won the war in 20 days.

By the second week of the war, the Syrians had been pushed entirely out of the Golan Heights. In the Sinai to the south, the Israelis struck at the "seam" between two invading Egyptian armies, crossed the Suez Canal (where the old cease fire line had been) and cut off the Egyptian Third Army just as the United Nations cease fire came into effect.

Five years later at the Camp David Accords were signed by Egyptian President Anwar el Sadat and Israeli Prime Minister Menachem Begin on September 17th, 1978 following 12 days of secret negotiations at Camp David in the U.S.A. The two agreements were signed at the White House and were witnessed by United States President Jimmy Carter. The Accords led directly to the 1979 Israel Egypt Peace Treaty.

Chapter 13

ISRAEL'S IMMIGRATION

The population of Israel has continued growing from its inception in 1948 to the present day making the verses in the Bible come true: Ezekiel 36:24: *"I will take you from every nation and country and bring you back to your own land."*

Three million people have immigrated to Israel since 1948.

The Bible says in Deuteronomy 30:1-5, *"I now give you a choice between a blessing and a curse. When all these things have happened to you, and you are living among the nations, where the Lord your God has scattered you, you will remember the choice I gave you. If you and your descendants will turn back to the Lord and with all your heart obey his commands that I am giving you today, then the Lord your God will have mercy on you. He will bring you back from the nations where he has scattered you, and he will make you prosperous again. Even if you are scattered to the farthest corners of the earth, the Lord your God will gather you together and bring you back, so that you may again take possession of the land where your ancestors once lived. And he will make you more prosperous and more numerous that your ancestors ever were."*

More than one million immigrants have arrived

since 1990. 950,000 came from the former Soviet Union; 157,000 people living in Israel were born in Morocco; 110,000 are from Romania; 77,000 are originally North American; 70,000 from Iraq; 70,000 from Ethiopia and 64,000 from Poland.

Zechariah 8:7-8, *"I will rescue my people from the lands where they have been taken, and will bring them back from east and west to live in Jerusalem. They will be my people, and I will be their God, ruling over them faithfully and justly"*.

Every day more and more Jews are returning to their homeland. Christians, who have read the Bible and know that this is God's will have formed many organizations which are helping the Jews to come back to Israel from the four corners of the world such as the Ebenezer Emergency Fund, Operation Exodus, Christians for Israel, Operation Aliyah and Christian Zionism to name a few. The Bible says in Isaiah 43:5-7, *"Do not be afraid – I am with you! "From the distant east and the farthest west, I will bring your people home. I will tell the north to let them go and the south not to hold them back. Let my people return from distant lands, from every part of the world. They are my people, and I created them to bring me glory."*

They could be afraid to come into a country that receives so many rocket attacks from the Arab world. Israel has to live with terrorism daily. They are in the news every week, but the Jews keep coming.

At the beginning of 2008, the population of Israel reached 7,241,000 residents.

5,472,000 – 75.6% are Jewish;
1,449,000 – 20% are Arab and
320,000 – 4.4% are 'others' (Christians and of no religion).

The Jews and non-Arabs who were not born in Israel number 1,930,000.

In 2007 new immigrants were 18,000 and 149,400 babies were born; in 2006 the immigrants were 14,880 and 109,120 babies were born.

One-quarter of the Israeli population live either in Jerusalem, Tel Aviv, Haifa or Rishon Letzion.

Among Israel's 14 largest cities is Rishon Letzion founded in the 1880s, which has grown from 11,000 residents in 1948 to 219,500 in 2007. Its neighbouring towns to the south: Rehovot, Ashkelon and Ashdod have grown in population.

Be'er Sheva, "capital of the Negev" and the largest city in the south, had 183,200 residents in 2003. The third largest city in the country, and the largest city in the north, is Haifa, with 267,000 people.

Of the country's Jewish and non-Arab population, 65 percent were born in Israel. In 1948, only 35 percent of Jews were born in the country.

(Above information obtained from the Jewish Virtual Library)

Jeremiah 31:36, *"He promises that as long as the natural order lasts, so long will Israel be a nation.*

If we want the natural order to last, we better pray that Israel remains a nation!

Chapter 14

HURRICANE KATRINA

The Americans forced Israel to give up the Gaza strip to have peace so in Aug. 15, 2005, the withdrawal of some 8,000 Israeli settlers from the Jewish community in Gush Katif in Gaza began. Two years earlier, Sharon had announced his plan for Israel's unilateral withdrawal from the Gaza Strip. Israel was to hold on to large blocks of land in the West Bank and reject the "right of return" for Palestinian refugees. The Israeli evacuation involved 21 Gaza settlements as well as four of the isolated West Bank's 120 settlements. Gaza, which has the world's highest population density, gained 25% more land and plans on replacing the settlers' single-family houses with apartment buildings to alleviate a severe housing shortage. A private group of American philanthropists purchased 800 acres of greenhouses from the departing settlers and donated them to the Palestinians, preserving an important source of jobs and revenue in an area with 40% unemployment. The majority of former Katif Jewish residents are currently homeless.

RESULT : On August 28th, 2005, Hurricane Katrina hit the southern coast of the United States with devastating effect.@ It was reported that more than 1,800 people lost their lives, and more then $81 billion dollars in damages occurred.

These are the similarities[2]:

1) Close to 10,000 Jews were expelled from their homes in the Gaza Strip and parts of northern Samaria. Katrina's death toll is now expected to reach at least 10,000.

2) America's population ratio to Israel is about 50:1. 10,000 Jews who lost their Gaza homes is the equivalent of about 500,000 Americans who are now reported to be displaced as a result of Katrina.

3) Gaza's Jewish communities were located in Israel's southern coastal region; Part of America's southern coastal region was ruined.

4) The Israeli government, backed by statements from U.S. Officials, demanded Gaza residents to evacuate their homes. The U.S. government called on Louisiana residents to evacuate their homes ahead of the storm.

5) President Bush from Texas and Condoleezza Rice from Alabama were the most vocal U.S. backers of the Gaza evacuation. Hurricane Katrina hit the states in between Texas and Alabama: Louisiana and Mississippi.

6) Similarity in scenes: Many residents of Jewish Gaza climbed to their rooftops to

escape the threat of expulsion, while the residents of the Gulf Coast climbed on their own rooftops to protect themselves from the rising waters.

7) Jewish Gaza homes described as beautiful and charming were demolished by Israel's military. The once beautiful homes in New Orleans now lie in ruins.

8) The day Katrina hit, Israel began carrying out what was termed the most controversial aspect of the Gaza withdrawal – the uprooting of bodies from the area's cemetery. There have been media reports of corpses floating around in flooded New Orleans regions.

9) Citizens of Israel were barred from entering Gush Katif; As Katrina was making landfall, U.S. Authorities barred citizens from entering the affected areas.

10) Gush Katif was an important agricultural area for Israel providing the Jewish State with 70% of its produce. A New Orleans port that exported much of the Midwest's agricultural production was destroyed by Hurricane Katrina.

11) When one looks at pictures of the destroyed Jewish houses in Gaza with the result of destroyed houses by Hurricane

Katrina, the photos could be interchanged. Very curious!

12) Even the names as Barry Chamish sent an e-mail noting, "Gush is like Gulf, and KATif is like KATrina.

If you take 'KAT' from KATif and KATrina, you are left with 'if' and 'rain'. If you support the Gush Katif evacuation, it will rain."

"I will curse those who curse you."

Is this just a coincidence?

Chapter 15

JERUSALEM

The Bible is full of quotes mentioning Jerusalem. Below are 5 of them:

The prophet Zechariah wrote in chapter 12:1-5.

"This is a message about Israel from the Lord, the Lord who spread out the skies, created the earth, and gave life to man. He says, "I will make Jerusalem like a cup of wine; the nations round her will drink and stagger like drunken men. And when they besiege Jerusalem, the cities of the rest of Judah will also be besieged. But when that time comes, I will make Jerusalem like a heavy stone – any nation that tries to lift it will be hurt. All the nations of the world join forces to attack her. At that time I will terrify all their horses and make all their riders go mad. I will watch over the people of Judah, but I will make the horses of their enemies blind. Then the clans of Judah will say to themselves, "The Lord God Almighty gives strength to his people who live in Jerusalem."

Zechariah 12:6, *At that time I will make the clans of Judah like a fire in a forest or in a field of ripe corn – they will destroy all the surrounding nations. The people of Jerusalem will remain safe in the city."*

Zechariah 12:8-9, *"At that time the Lord will protect those who live in Jerusalem and even the weakest* among them will become as strong as David was. The descendants of David will lead them like the angel of the Lord, like God himself. At that time I will destroy every nation that tries to attack Jerusalem."

Zachariah 12:10, *"I will fill the descendants of David and the other people of Jerusalem with the spirit of mercy and the spirit of prayer. They will look at the one whom they stabbed to death, and they will mourn for him like those who mourn for an only child. They will mourn bitterly, like those who have lost their firstborn son.*

In Isaiah 62:12 the Bible says, *"You will be called "God's Holy people", "The People the Lord has Saved." Jerusalem will be called "The City that God loves",* "The City that God did not Forsake."

Chapter 16

60ᵀᴴ BIRTHDAY PARTY

Queen Victoria asked Disraeli, the Prime Minister at the time, "Tell me 3 words that confirm that God exists." He replied, "I can prove that to you in one word: Jew."

In our lifetime there have been many attempts to get rid of the Jews with no success.

The Bible says in Genesis 12:1-3, *"The Lord said to Abram, "Leave your country, your relatives and your father's home, and go to a land that I am going to show you. I will give you many descendants, and they will become a great nation. I will bless you and make your name famous, so that you will be a blessing."*

I will bless those who bless you, But I will curse those who curse you. And through you I will bless all the nations.

Abram obeyed God and left Haran as the Lord had told him.

This year Israel will be 60 years old and is very prosperous even though she is surrounded by enemies.

The blessing was with Israel as having less than a million people they fought all the Arab countries which wanted to eliminate the State of Israel and won and is still winning even though the Arab countries which surround them are extremely rich and can buy many weapons.

Reading through the Bible one can say that Israel is the land of miracles:

1) The fall of the walls in Jericho
2) The people walking on dry ground crossing the River Jordan under Joshua's leadership and the waters returning when all the Israelites had all crossed over.
3) The sun standing still until the Israelites had won the battle under Joshua's leadership.
4) Jonah being spewed by a whale into the beach
5) David beating the giant Goliath with a sling and a stone
6) The poor woman pouring oil into jars that kept on filling until the jars were all full and she could have enough money to pay her dead husband's debts and she had enough money for her and her two sons to live on.
7) Elisha making the water pure with salt and a prayer.
8) Naaman being healed of leprosy by bathing in the River Jordan seven times.
9) Elisha making the iron axe to float so the man could return it as it was borrowed.

10) Gideon getting victory over the Midianites with only 300 men (and obviously God's help)

11) The sun going back 10 steps for King Hezekiah to know that God will keep His word and live 15 years longer,

Etc., etc., etc.

In our life time we have witnessed the news on how Israel won 3 wars against all odds in 1948, 1967 and 1973.

Chapter 17

THANKFULNESS

In the letter of Paul to the Romans, he explains the Jews in these words: Romans 9:4-5, *"They are God's people; he made them his children and revealed his glory to them; he made his covenants with them and gave them the Law; they have the true worship; they have received God's promises; they are descended from the famous Hebrew ancestors;* and Christ, as a human being, belongs to their race. *May God, who rules over all, be praised for ever! Amen.*

In the same letter to the Romans, Paul asks a question: Romans 11:1-6, *"I ask then: did God reject his own people? Certainly not! I myself am an Israelite, a descendant of Abraham, a member of the tribe of Benjamin. God has not rejected his people, whom he chose from the beginning. You know what the scripture says in the passage where Elijah pleads with God against Israel: "Lord, they have killed your prophets and torn down your altars; I am the only one left, and they are trying to kill me." What answer did God give him? "I have kept for myself seven thousand men who have not worshipped the false god Baal." It is the same way now; there is a small number left of those whom God has chosen because of his grace. His choice is based on his grace, not on what they have* done. *For if God's choice were based on what people do, then his grace would not be real grace."*

Paul continues to explain in Romans 11:25-29, *"There is a secret truth, my brothers and sisters, which I want you to know, for it will keep you from thinking how wise you are. It is that the stubbornness of the people of Israel is not permanent, but will last only until the complete number of Gentiles comes to God. And this is how all Israel will be saved. As the scripture says:*

"The Saviour will come from Zion and remove all wickedness from the descendants of Jacob. I will make this covenant with them when I take away their sins."

Because they reject the Good News, the Jews are God's enemies for the sake of you Gentiles. But because of God's choice, they are his friends because of their ancestors. For God does not change his mind about whom he chooses and blesses."

This is why the gentiles should be thankful to the Jews for their salvation.

The Bible says in Psalm 122:6, **"Pray for the peace of Jerusalem: "May those who love you prosper."**

Chapter 18

RETURN OF JESUS
TO JERUSALEM

Jesus came to teach us how to live and because God loved us so much, God sent Him to die to pay for our sins in Calvary. God raised Jesus on the third day and 40 days later, Jesus ascended into heaven from Jerusalem and will return the same way he was raised to Jerusalem because the Bible says in Acts 1:6-11, *"When the apostles met together with Jesus, they asked him, "Lord, will you at this time give the Kingdom back to Israel? Jesus said to them, "The times and occasions are set by my Father's own authority, and it is not for you to know when they will be. But when the Holy Spirit comes upon you, you will be filled with power, and you will be witnesses for me in Jerusalem, in all Judea and Samaria, and to the ends of the earth. After saying this, he was taken up to heaven as they watched him, and a cloud hid him from their sight. They still had their eyes fixed on the sky as he went away, when two men dressed in white suddenly stood beside them and said, "Galileans, why are you standing there looking up at the sky? This Jesus, who was taken from you into heaven, will come back in the same way that you saw him go to heaven."*

94

Therefore the Jews have to be living in Jerusalem to welcome Jesus back. The enemy of God, Satan, has encouraged Israel's neighbours to go to war to accomplish this. There have been 3 major wars:

15th May 1948 – the day after their re-birth

1st June 1967 – the day the Jews had control of the whole of Jerusalem after the 6th day war

6th October 1973 – when a coalition of Arab states attacked Israel on its most sacred feast – Yom Kippur – which is the day of atonement. Israel won more land, but they have been forced to give up some land in the name of peace. No other country has been forced to give up land gained during a war paid by the blood of their people.

Comparing their strength, Israel had no chance of winning (see pages 71, 74 and 77), but God was on their side and they won.

Many Arab Musti, (their religious leaders) continue to urge for the extinction of Israel. This will never happen as the Bible says in Psalm 89:35-37, *"Once and for all I have promised by my holy name: I will never lie to David. He will always have descendants, and I will watch over his kingdom* **as long as the sun shines.**

It will be as permanent as the moon, that faithful witness in the sky."

The last book of the Bible called Revelation described exactly how Jesus will come: Revelation 19:11, *"Then I saw heaven open, and there was a white horse. Its rider is called Faithful and True; it is with justice that he judges and fights his battles."*

The Bible explains what is going to happen when Jesus comes, in the last chapter and the last book of the Bible. Revelation 22:12-17, *"Listen! Says Jesus. "I am coming soon! I will bring my rewards with me, to give to each one according to what he has done. I am the first and the last, the beginning and the end."*

Happy are those who wash their robes clean and so have the right to eat the fruit from the tree of life and to go through the gates into the city. But outside the city are the perverts and those who practise magic, the immoral and the murderers, those who worship idols and those who are liars both in words and deeds."

It is very interesting that a person who lies is considered just as sinful as one who commits murder. That means that no one is righteous so we all need to accept that Jesus paid the price for our sins. Have you lied? Then you need

Jesus as your Saviour otherwise you will not be allowed into the Holy City.

The Book of Revelation continues in chapter 22 verse 16, *"I, Jesus, have sent my angel to announce these things to you in the churches. I am descended from the family of David; I am the bright morning star." The Spirit and the Bride say, "Come!"*

Everyone who hears this must also say, "Come!"

Come, whoever is thirsty; accept the water of life as a gift, whoever wants it."

The Bible ends with these words: Revelation 22:20-21, *"He who gives his testimony to all this says, "Yes indeed! I am coming soon!"*

So be it. Come, Lord Jesus!

May the grace of the Lord Jesus be with everyone."

NOTES

Note 1 : *Chapter 10* – **State of Israel.** The information from the Bible calculating the exact day when Israel would be reborn was explained on God TV by Rory Alec quoting a book written by someone. Sorry do not know the author.

Note 2 : *Chapter 14* – **Hurricane Katrina.** Information was obtained from Jewish Voice Today November/December 2005 article titled "Did God send Katrina as Revenge over Gaza?" pages 6,7,15 written by guest Author Aaron Klein.

Note 3: I researched most of the information written in this book using **Google, the Jewish Virtual Library and Wikipedia.**

With Grateful Thanks

APPENDIX

Quotations from the Bible

Chapter 1 **Blessings and Curses**	Genesis 12:1-2 Genesis 12:3 Genesis 12:7-9 Genesis 13:14-18 Genesis 14:14-16 Genesis 14:17-20 Genesis 15:7 Genesis 15:13-16 Genesis 15:17-20
Chapter 2 **Abraham, Isaac and Jacob**	Genesis 17:7-8 Genesis 17:19 Genesis 17:20 Genesis 17:21 Genesis 21:30-34 Genesis 22:2 Genesis 22:9-12 Genesis 22:13 Genesis 23:17 Genesis 26:1-5 Genesis 28:13-15 Genesis 32:28
Chapter 3 **Joseph**	Genesis 49:10

Chapter 4 **Moses**	Genesis 15:16
Chapter 5 **Extermination**	Esther 10:3 Esther 9:25... 2 Chronicles 20:15-17
Chapter 6 **Jesus**	Matthew 1-17 Isaiah 53:3-81 Peter 22:25 Luke 23:34 Luke 24:6-7 Matthew 28:5-10 John 3:16-17 Luke 19:43-44 Luke 21:24
Chapter 7 **Expulsions of the Jews**	Deuteronomy 28:32
Chapter 9 **People**	Genesis 12:3
Chapter 10 **State of Israel**	Ezekiel 4:1 Leviticus 26:23-24 Amos 9:11 Amos 9:15
Chapter 11 **6 – Day War**	Amos 9:15
Chapter 12 **Yom Kippur War**	Leviticus 23:27-28

Chapter 13 **Israel's Immigration**	Ezekiel 36:24 Deuteronomy 30:1-5 Zechariah 8:7-8 Isaiah 43:5-7 Jeremiah 31:36
Chapter 15 **Jerusalem**	Zechariah 12:1-5 Zechariah 12:6 Zechariah 12:8-9 Zechariah 12:8-9
Chapter 16 **60ᵗʰ Birthday Party**	Genesis 12:1-3
Chapter 17 **Thankfulness**	Romans 9:4-5 Romans 11:1-6 Romans 11:25-29 Psalm 122:6
Chapter 18 **Return of Jesus to Jerusalem**	Acts 1:6-11 Psalm 89:35-37 Revelation 19:11 Revelation 19:19-21 Revelation 22:12-17 Revelation 22: 20-21